# Christians!

## Their Message and their Witness

## Brian Sherring

ISBN: 978-1-78364-476-6

The Open Bible Trust
Fordland Mount, Upper Basildon,
Reading, RG8 8LU, UK.

www.obt.org.uk

# Christians!

## Their Message and their Witness

## Contents

*****

# Preface

When I first began to study the Bible as a young believer, I was somewhat surprised at the almost total absence of the word "Christian" in the New Testament—only three references. And yet the word was much used in the church I attended and in Christian circles generally. Of course, we were always careful to make clear what we considered constituted a Christian, since the word was used in secular society of anyone who lived a good life. Also, in those days, Great Britain (e.g.) was described as a "Christian Nation", an expression if used today, would probably be considered politically (as well as factually) incorrect.

In this book I look at the origin and meaning of the word "Christian" and the apparent reluctance, at first, of the early believers to accept it as a word to describe themselves. I consider also the use of the word "saints" to describe believers, the message they preached and believed, and their consequent witness in word and life.

One of the dictionary meanings of the word "Christian" is, "a decent, respectable person" (*Chambers Concise*): I trust that this booklet will dispel any notion that the word has ever been exhausted by that definition, reminding us that the first six letters of the word spell **"Christ"**, and that without Him and His sacrifice for our sins, the word is meaningless.

The dates of New Testament events given in the text are taken from *Biblical Chronology* by Dr. Peter John - Charles (obtainable from The Open Bible Trust – **www.obt.org.uk**).

# Chapter 1: Christians

## What's in a Name?

In Shakespeare's *Romeo and Juliet*, Juliet poses the question, "What's in a name?" She states that it is not the **name** but the **nature** of the person or thing that matters—"That which we call a rose, *by any other name* would smell as sweet" (Act 2 scene 2). This is certainly true in everyday affairs, but when we come to study the way names are used in the Scriptures there is more to it than this. Names are not given arbitrarily and if we had any doubts about this, we have only to recall the emphasis that is given to "**the name** that is above every name" before which "every knee should bow" (Philippians 2:9,10). It is not just bowing before the person of Jesus, but bowing before His name.

We meet with the importance of names on the first pages of Scripture, where although the creation is described in just two chapters, the narrator still finds space to note that the Lord

*Christians: Their Message and their Witness 5*

God brought "all the beasts of the field and all the birds of the air" to Adam, "to see what he would *name them*; and whatever the man called each living creature, *that was its name*" (Genesis 2:19). The narrator also states that God "also made the stars", introducing this stupendous event almost as an afterthought, but later the Psalmist declares, "He determines the number of the stars; *he gives to all of them their names*" (147:4 *ESV*). (The implications of this are too complicated to introduce into a booklet of this nature; the interested reader might like to obtain Dr. E.W. Bullinger's book *The Witness of the Stars* (obtainable from OBT) where the actual names of the stars are seen to have been of great significance to the ancients and give point to the fact that it was *God that named them*.)

Abram (meaning 'exalted father') had his name changed by the Lord to Abraham (meaning 'father of a multitude') reflecting the position that he was to have in the purpose of God—"I have made you a father of many nations" (Genesis 17:5). Isaac (connected to the Hebrew 'laugh') looks back to when Abraham *laughed* at the thought of he and Sarah having a child at their advanced ages (Genesis 17:17; 21:1-8). The name Jacob ('heel catcher') reflected the fact that at his birth he took hold of his twin brother Esau's heel and was prophetic of his 'grasping' (through guile) both Esau's birthright and blessing (Genesis 25:21-34; 27:1-40).

In the New Testament, and particularly in the early part of Acts, the importance of one name is forcefully made. **The name** is of course, "Jesus of Nazareth", made "both Lord and Christ", in whose **name** the early Christians were baptized for the forgiveness of sins, in whose **name** the crippled beggar is healed. It was in that same **name** that Peter and John were commanded by the priests and Sadducees "not to speak or teach", but most important of all, and as Peter testified to the Jews, "There is **no other name** under heaven given to men by which we must be saved" (Acts 2:22,36-38; 3:16; 4:10,12,18). And, reminding ourselves again as a final example, looking forward to that future day when all in heaven and on earth give to Him who has that name, the honour and worship due to Him, "God exalted him to the highest place and gave him **the name that is above every name**, that at **the name of Jesus** every knee should bow" (Philippians 2:9,10).

The truth that Peter declared before the Sanhedrin in Acts 4:12, is just as relevant today; "Salvation is found in no-one else…. there is **no other name**"—the name of Jesus Christ. None of us can pronounce judgement upon our fellow man and say that they are not saved, but we can stand by this truth. It is the salvation offered to all in the **name** of Jesus Christ that will define all our futures, whatever our colour, creed, religion or status in life—there is no other way and no other name.

In the light of the emphasis placed by the early believers on the name Jesus Christ, it seems strange that they seemed at first to be reluctant to call themselves "Christians". Not once, as we shall see, was it "used by Christians of themselves in the New Testament" (F.F. Bruce

*Commentary on the Acts of the Apostles*). Why was this?

## "Christian": Its Earliest Usage

We would not expect the word "Christian" to be used in the Old Testament, or perhaps in the Gospels, which cover only three to four years of Christ's life, but Luke tells us in the sequel to his Gospel, *The Acts of the Apostles*, that:

> The disciples were called Christians first at Antioch (in Syria). (11:26)

This was about A.D. 43. Barnabas had just been to Tarsus to fetch Saul (still called at this time by his Hebrew name) whose conversion had taken place some seven years earlier (John-Charles) – Acts 9. They were to minister there for "a whole year" (11:25,26). Antioch in Syria was the third largest city of the Roman Empire (after Rome and Alexandria). Some of those scattered by the persecution that followed the death of the first martyr to the faith, Stephen, had travelled there, and they had "spoken to the Hellenists also, telling them the good news about the Lord Jesus" (*ESV*). F.F. Bruce notes that it was the location where "The first use of *ekklesia* (church) in Acts (was used) for a community other than the original Jerusalem church either in its pristine unity or in dispersion".

When the number of the disciples of Jesus Christ began to increase—3000...5000 (Acts 2:41; 4:4), outsiders looked upon these Jewish believers as just another Jewish sect. And there was every reason to do so, for they continued to go into the temple at the hour of prayer, circumcised their male children and obeyed the Law of Moses; they were known as "the Nazarene sect" (Acts 3:1; 16:1-3; 21:17-26; 24:1-8). Since Pentecost they had also been known as those who belonged to "the Way" (9:1,2; 19:9) and were variously spoken of as brothers, disciples, believers and saints, but not for some time as "Christians". In modern parlance this might imply, "partisans of Christ".

As a Jewish sect, they would be included under the official Roman policy of religious tolerance that was extended to the Jews as a whole. At first believers were mainly Jews, proselytes and God-fearers who attached themselves to Judaism. It was when "a great many people were added to the Lord" (Acts 11:21), becoming believers in Christ in large numbers, that they took on an identity distinct from the unbelieving Jews. It was then that Luke recorded, "the disciples were called Christians first at Antioch".

## The Word "Christianois"

The Greek word *Christos*, Christ, from which *Christianois*, Christians, is derived is equivalent to the Hebrew *Messiah* and means literally 'anointed'. It came to be used as a personal name of Jesus rather than as a title. Unbelieving Gentiles confused it with *chrestos*, 'good', 'kind', 'useful'. See its usage in Ephesians 4:32, "Be *kind* and compassionate to one another" and 1 Peter 2:3, "You have tasted that the Lord is *good*". Possibly (and hopefully) this confusion came about because these early Christians exhibited the qualities resident in the word *chrestos*.

We cannot be certain whether the term "Christians" (*Christianois*) was adopted by the disciples themselves or made up by their enemies as a term of reproach, but I think the latter to be more likely. In either case, as Peter wrote later, "If you suffer as a *Christian*, do not be ashamed, but praise God that you bear that name" (1 Peter 4:16). It was nothing to be ashamed of and yet it is not used by believers of themselves in the New Testament.

Of the three occurrences of the word, Luke simply records that it was at Antioch that they were first called Christians, without saying who it was that called them that. And the way he put it suggests that it was 'outsiders' that referred to them as such, otherwise why did he not say, "the disciples first *called themselves* Christians at Antioch"? Likewise, standing before Agrippa, it is *not* Paul who uses the word, but the king who says: "Do you think that in such a short time you can persuade me to be *a Christian*?" (*NIV*), or as *Moffatt* puts it, "At this rate … It won't be long before you believe you have made *a Christian* of me" (Acts 26:28). And in the third occurrence (1Peter 4:16) Peter is contrasting being accused of being a murdere*r, a thief or a criminal (v.15), with being *accused* of being a Christian; it is the language of the court of law and the word "Christian" is on the lips of the accuser.

## Early Reluctance to use the Word

Believers seem to have been reluctant to use the name "Christian" in the 1st century. Paul never uses the word, even in his later epistles. In other early Christian writings (admittedly they are scant) it does not appear until the Epistles of Ignatius to seven churches, written by him early 2nd century. He refers to "the company of those *Christians* of Ephesus" (*Ephesians* 11) and in his other epistles wrote,

It is therefore meet that we not only be called *Christians*, but also be such. (*Magnesians* 4)

Pray.... that I may not only be called a *Christian*, but also be found one (*Romans* 3).

A *Christian* hath no authority over himself, but giveth his time to God. (*to Polycarp* 7)

A document giving an account of *The Martyrdom of Polycarp* (AD 155/156) refers to the "bravery (under torture) of the God-beloved and God-fearing people of *the Christians*" (3). Polycarp, bishop of Smyrna in Asia Minor (circa 69-155), is recognised as an important link between the first–generation Apostles and the theologians of the late 2nd century. Called upon to revile Christ he said, "I am, hear thou plainly, I am *a Christian*" and was later condemned because he "confessed himself to be *a Christian*". Both Jews and Gentiles who had gathered to witness his martyrdom cried out, "This is the teacher of Asia, the father of *the Christians*, the puller down of our gods" (9-12).

Tertullian (circa 160-240), a lawyer brought up in Carthage (Tunisia) as a pagan, was converted to Christianity when he lived for some time in Rome. He wrote in defence of his new faith in a work we know as his *Apology*, condemning the authorities for their treatment of "the Christians". He wrote: "This, then, is the first plea we lodge with you – the injustice of your hatred of *the Christian name*" (1.4). Later he goes on, "Tell me…. if it is hatred of a name, how can you indict names?…. you have not even certain knowledge of the mere name". He chides them for mispronouncing the word as "Chrestian", rather than "Christian", and complains that the guardians of the law cut the case short by saying to the Christian in the dock, "Your existence is illegal" (3.5: 4.3,4).

There are references to "Christians" in early non-Christian writings by Josephus in *The Antiquities of the Jews* (18.3.3, completed about AD 93); Suetonius (*The Twelve Caesars*), a Latin biographer, who wrote in the early 2$^{nd}$ century; Pliny the Younger. a prominent Roman lawyer (AD 62-113) in a letter to Trajan, and Tacitus (circa 60-120) the Roman historian. The last named summed up the general attitude to the "Christians" at the time when he spoke of them as "a class hated for their abominations, who are *commonly called Christians*".

Such was the fanatical hatred that came to be associated with the name "Christian" by the middle of the 2$^{nd}$ century, but by this time believers seemed to have thoroughly accepted the name and were proud to suffer for the One from whom it was derived.

## Who First Coined The Name?

It seems that the description of the followers of Christ as "Christians" may first have been coined by unbelievers and was only adopted much later by the Christians themselves. It was "disciples" who were first called Christians, and a disciple in the New Testament was a *follower* of Christ.

These were not people interested only in the teaching of Christ from an academic point of view, but *followers* who put that teaching into practice, who *followed* Christ in both word and deed, and often had to suffer for their beliefs.

As a description of believers, the word "Christian" is first associated with a church in Syria (Antioch), where there were a great number of Greek speaking Jews (*Hellenistas*; Acts 11:19-20, *ESV*).

Barnabas and Paul spent a whole year there teaching "great numbers of people". Almost certainly unbelieving Gentiles would have coined the word, since unbelieving Jews would hardly have associated this 'sect' with the Messiah (Christ), the One they still looked for. On the basis of the evidence we have, both scriptural and secular, it seems that believers were slow to identify themselves with the word "Christian", but when they eventually did, they were proud to be called such, and willing to accept the persecution that so often followed the confession of the name.

# Paul and "Christians"

Paul could have had no doubt to whom Agrippa was referring when he stood before the king (A.D.60) and the king said to him, "At this rate ... It won't be long before you believe you have made *a Christian* of me" (Acts 26:28 *Moffatt*). It was the king who used the word, not Paul. And even as late as A.D. 67, when 2 Timothy was written (John-Charles) he has still not referred to believers as such. This is some twenty-four years after its first usage in Antioch. Paul preferred to use the words "saints" or "brothers" when referring to believers and the name "Christians" is not found in any (surviving) letter of his.

I do not like drawing conclusions from negatives, but the almost complete absence of the word in the New Testament, and especially in Paul's writings, is so strange that it demands an answer. We can postulate that Paul, who together with others seems not to have used the word of themselves, was too conscious of its origin—coined by unbelievers, but there is another suggestion that is worth considering. The nearest Paul came to referring to believers as "Christians" was when he referred to one of the factions in the Corinthian church who were saying, "I follow Christ". Look at it in context:

> My brothers, some from Chloe's household have informed me that there are quarrels among you. What I mean is this: One of you says, "I follow Paul"; another, "I follow Apollos"; another, "I follow Cephas"; still another, "*I follow Christ*". Is Christ divided? (1 Corinthians 1:11-13)

At first reading it might seem that those who claimed to "follow Christ" were in the right and were to be commended, and the rest were wrong, but Paul does not look at it like this. This was partisanship and it produced divisions among the believers in Corinth. Some claimed to be the Paul party, probably because he first taught them; some followed Apollos, admired for his learning and knowledge of the Old Testament Scriptures (Acts 18:24; 19:1); others followed Cephas (Peter) leader of The Twelve Apostles and some said, "I (am) of Christ" (lit). It seems unlikely that these parties had different teachings, since Paul does not condemn them for this; what he is concerned about is the fact that there **are** such parties. *In such a context* to say "I belong to Christ" is just as much to be condemned as "I belong to Paul" etc. It is divisive. Did they not all "follow Christ"? "Is Christ divided?"

The Greeks and the Romans were great admirers of men of wisdom (cp. 1 Corinthians 1:18-22) and were proud to be identified with them under names like, for example, Pythagoreans (followers of Pythagoras the 6th century Greek philosopher). The partisanship that came about within the church in Corinth was just an extension of this, and the party that claimed "I am (or belong to) Christ", has to be seen in this context. It was a superior claim over their brethren who were merely "of Paul" or "of Apollos" etc. Did they not all belong to Christ? And while the word is not used here, this party were not that far away from taking on the name "Christians" in distinction from their fellow believers. Paul could not tolerate this.

The problem of partisanship is still evident in Paul's second epistle to the same church, where the exclusiveness suggested by the claim "**I** follow (or belong to) Christ" is suggested by his words: "If anyone is confident that *he belongs to Christ*, he should consider again that *we belong to Christ just as much as he*" (10:7). To claim to belong to Christ in distinction from other brethren, be it Paul himself, his colleagues or others within the Corinthian church, was a boast that Paul condemned, especially since it detracted from the fellowship that should exist between all believers. All, whether taught by Paul, Apollos or Peter, belonged to Christ; He was *the foundation* of the church upon which others built (1 Corinthians 3:11). So Paul chose to refer to believers in other terms, even though the term "Christian" had been coined many years before:

> To all in Rome who are loved by God and called to be **saints**. (Romans 1:7)

To the church of God in Corinth, to those *sanctified* in Christ Jesus and called to be holy, together with all those everywhere who call on the name of our Lord Jesus Christ—their Lord and ours. (1 Corinthians 1:2)

To the **saints** in Ephesus, the faithful in Christ Jesus. (Ephesians 1:1)

How much simpler it would have been to have written, "to the Christians in Rome … in Corinth … in Ephesus", but Paul doesn't do so.

## Christians as "Saints"

In the New Testament believers are called "saints" many times, especially by Paul, and, contrary to what we might at first expect, the word is used also many times in the Old Testament. In modern usage "saint" has three basic meanings: 1) The Catholic and Orthodox churches use it of "a person formally recognised or canonised by the Church after death, who may be the object of veneration" (*Oxford English Dictionary*). 2) It is sometimes used simply of a very good person ("she's a saint") and 3) in biblical usage it is used of believers in general. The link between the Old and New Testaments provided by the Greek translation of the former (*Septuagint LXX*), is helpful in establishing who the Jews of old considered to be "saints" and provides the background against which the New Testament references may be understood.

## "Saints" in the Old Testament

In English versions of the Old Testament the word "saints" occurs mostly in the Psalms and is the translation of two basic Hebrew words, *qadosh* and *chasid*. The difference of meaning between these words (unrelated in etymology) seems to be that *qadosh* refers to one who has been set apart, separated, and *chasid* emphasises the manner of life such a one should lead. The two ideas are resident in Psalm 4:3, "The LORD has *set apart* the godly (*chasid*) for himself", where the word rendered "set apart" (*palah*) is

*Christians: Their Message and their Witness* 23

the same as that used for the "*distinction* between Egypt and Israel" made by the Lord at the time of the exodus (Exodus 11:7). This compares with Paul's exhortation in the New Testament, addressed to "the *saints* and faithful in Christ Jesus", where the "saints" are urged to be faithful and "live a life worthy of the calling received" (Ephesians 1:1; 4:1). Hence the two sides of being a "saint" come together in that God has *set them apart* (the believer's calling and position in Christ) but expects *the believers response* (walk worthy).

Both words suggest 'holiness' and *qadosh* in particular is translated many times "holy" in association with other words, so, "*holy* nation", "*holy* place", "*holy* people" etc. It is used many times in Isaiah of "*the Holy One* of Israel". The word is not, therefore, exclusive to humans, for, apart from its use of God, it is also used of spirit beings (angels) at the giving of the Law (Hebrews 2:2 with Deuteronomy 33:2) "The LORD came from Sinai … with myriads of *holy ones*". (See also Psalm 89:5-7.) A "saint" in the Old Testament, when referred to humans, was one separated to God and called upon to live a life worthy of that privilege and responsibility.

In its widest sense *qadosh* was used of Israel *as a nation*, who were separated by the Lord from the other nations in order to effect His purpose for the earth. They were His chosen people who were to be a blessing to all peoples on earth (Genesis 12:1-3). As such they were not only separated, but also expected to show that they were His special people by the lives they led. He commanded them, "Consecrate yourselves and be holy (*qadosh*), because I (the LORD your God) am holy (*qadosh*)" (Leviticus 11:44).

## Saint (*hagios*) in the New Testament

The word used by the Greek version of the Old Testament to translate the Hebrew words for "saint" is *hagios*. It is used many times in the New Testament, but outside of the epistles of Paul not often of believers as "saints". In the *King James Version* it is rendered "saints" over

60 times and in conjunction with *pneuma*, "*Holy Ghost (Spirit)*" over 90 times. Just as it was in the Old Testament, so likewise in the New, *hagios* was applied to spirit beings as well as to God and to humans. To demonstrate the usage of the word "saint" or "holy" (*hagios*) in the New Testament in any detail would take up many pages in this booklet, so for those interested I have given a brief summary of its usage in Appendix 1, using the *KJV* as a basis of translation.

The conclusions I draw from the usage of *hagios* in the New Testament, when referring to "saints", is that outside of Paul's epistles the "saints" are Jewish believers, and the use of the word to describe them so is but *a continuation of its usage in the Old Testament*. It describes one who is called, set apart, godly and faithful. But with the coming of the Messiah, that calling and separation was a call to respond to the Gospel of Christ, a Gospel that called for repentance and trust in His name—"Save yourselves from this corrupt generation" said Peter to his countrymen (Acts 2:40).

That call for the repentance of Israel was a constant theme of the Old Testament and was continued by John the Baptist, the Lord himself and His disciples in the early part of Acts (Matthew 3:1,2; 4:17; Acts 2:38). Paul however, uses the word 'saint' more widely to include believing Gentiles.

*Christians: Their Message and their Witness* 28

# Chapter 2: Christians: Then and Now

## The "Christian" Message

Reading through the early part of The Acts of the Apostles, it is evident that the message preached by the early "Christians", was different in some ways to that which we preach today. And this is not due solely to the distance in time. For a start, it was initially a witness to the Jewish nation, who still retained their special place in the purpose of God, in spite of their unbelief (Romans 11:1,2 cp. 9:1-5; 3:1,2). And there was common ground between preacher and hearers in that both held the Old Testament to be God's Word, so that what was preached could be tested against the touchstone of "the Scriptures" (Acts 2:16,25; 17:10-11 cp. 26:6-8,22).

There was also a different emphasis than there is in the Gentile world today. Then, it was to show that Jesus of Nazareth *is* the Christ, the long awaited Messiah of the Old Testament, that *He is* the Son of God (John 20:30,31; Acts 9:22), and that the proof was not only in the miracles He did, but also in the fact of His *resurrection*. He was "declared with power to be the Son of God, by his resurrection from the dead" (Romans 1:4). And there were still witnesses alive who could testify to His resurrection (1 Corinthians 15:6).

The implications of the resurrection of Christ, foreseen by David and fulfilled in Jesus of Nazareth (Acts 2:25-32) led (on the day of Pentecost) to Peter's call to his nation to repent and his plea to the Jews to, "Save yourselves from this corrupt generation" (2:38,40). It was a witness to a nation, to a people who, although still God's chosen people, had turned away from Him. They had rejected their Messiah and been responsible for His crucifixion; now they were given a second chance to accept Him, in response to the Lord 's Prayer, "Father, forgive them, for they do not know what they are doing" (Luke 23:34; Acts 3:13-17). That this witness (nationally) was largely refused is now history, but it led to a witness among the Gentiles that continues with us to this day, but a witness that is in some points different to the early preaching in the Acts.

Today, witnessing among unbelieving Gentiles, we cannot appeal to the Scriptures as common ground, since the Bible is not considered to be an authority by many (probably most) people. And we do not primarily try to show that Jesus **is** the Christ (except perhaps to a Jew) since our starting point assumes it, insofar that "Jesus Christ" is accepted wholly as a name, not a name and a title.   But the key factor in Christian witness has not changed; it is still a witness to Christ or Jesus Christ, or even "Jesus". And when witnessing to what He has done for us, we still maintain, "Salvation is found in no-one else, for there is no other *name* under heaven given to men by which we must be saved" (Acts 4:12). His resurrection is still the keystone upon which that salvation is built, "If Christ has not been raised, our preaching is useless and so is your faith … we are then found to be false witnesses … you are still in your sins" (1 Corinthians

15:12-17). Paul outlines the basis of our witness in 1 Corinthians 15:1-5:

> The gospel I preach … By this gospel you are saved … of first importance: that Christ died for our sins … that he was buried, that he was raised on the third day … and that he appeared to (various witnesses …).

In quoting this, I have left out the evidence that Paul in his day could appeal to, that this was "according to the (Old Testament) Scriptures" and that many still living at the time he wrote these words could verify the resurrection of Christ. Nevertheless, our belief that the New Testament claim, that He rose from the dead, relies initially on their testimony and without that assurance our faith in Him is in vain.

But, granted all the above, there is one further very important difference between the preaching of the early believers and their expectation, and what we today call the Gospel of Christ, and how Christians now understand "the hope of His calling". In order to appreciate this difference, let's look firstly at these early believers, their message, how they lived and what they hoped for.

## The Early Believers (Jews and Proselytes)

In order to understand who these early believers were and why they spoke and acted as they did, we cannot start with the record of The Acts of the Apostles, but must go back to the Gospels. We must remember that they had the Old Testament and its teaching ('the Scriptures' to them) as the background to their beliefs, and recall that the Lord did not sweep all this aside when He began to teach. He said,

> "Do not think that I have come to abolish the Law or the Prophets; I have not come to abolish them but *to fulfil them*. I tell you the truth, until heaven and earth disappear, not the smallest letter, not the least stroke of a pen, will by any means disappear from the

Law until everything is accomplished" (Matthew 5:17,18).

For at least three years He taught His disciples, making constant reference to these "Scriptures", and after His resurrection from the dead, to two of them on the road to Emmaus, "He *explained to them* what was said in all the Scriptures concerning himself". Later, to the Eleven, "He *opened their minds so they could understand* the Scriptures", assuring them that "Everything must be fulfilled that is written about me in the Law of Moses, the Prophets and the Psalms" (Luke 24:13-27,33,45,46). Over a period of forty days following His resurrection He spoke to them about the kingdom of God (Acts 1:3). At the end of this period they were gathered together on the Mount of Olives, and with these experiences and the Lord's teaching still in their minds they asked Him:

> "Lord, are you at this time going to *restore* the kingdom to Israel?" (Acts 1:6)

The key words in this question are, "at this time"; there was never any doubt that one day, the "kingdom", lost many years before to various Gentile nations, and at present under the dominion of Rome, would be restored to them. And the Lord's answer never suggested that that "restoration" would never take place, nor that they had misunderstood His teaching; the only thing that needed to be resolved was *when would it take place*—would it be "at this time"? So He said:

> It is not for you to know *the times or dates* the Father has set by his own authority (v.7)

Later on in Acts, Peter links that "restoration" to the second coming of Christ, who "must remain in heaven *until the time comes* for God to *restore* everything, as he promised long ago through his holy prophets" (Acts 3:20,21), and, as the Lord had taught them during His earthly ministry, "No-one knows about *that day or hour*, not even the angels in heaven, nor the Son, but only the Father" (Matthew 24:36). Standing on the Mount of Olives on the day of His ascension, the Son of

God is not unwilling, but *cannot* say when that day will be—only the Father knows.

Why was this kept secret from them; these were after all the Lord's own disciples? We can understand that He might withhold His truth from the ungodly, but not "His own". The answer, as I see it, is not that He is unwilling to make His secrets known to His people, but that there is a factor at work upon which "times and dates" depend—*the human factor.*

I cannot go into this in any detail here; interested readers will find it discussed at some length in Appendix 2 of my booklet *Introducing the Books of the Bible*.[1] Basically, it involves the fact that we have not been created as puppets, completely controlled by the strings of God, but as responsible people who can say 'No' just as much as 'Yes'. And while God's purposes will never be thwarted, the moral condition of those to whom prophecy is addressed, can and will, affect *when* that prophecy is fulfilled. So that,

_____

[1] Published The Open Bible Trust.

relating this 'factor' back to the position of the early believers, there was never any doubt that the Lord would return, and that all things spoken of in the Prophets would come to pass—what could not be said with any certainty from the human point of view, was *when*, for that was *conditional* upon the response of Peter's countrymen. And this *conditional factor* is evident in Peter's words to his people:

> Now brothers ... Repent, then, and turn to God ... that he may send the Christ, who has been appointed for you—even Jesus. He must remain in heaven until the time comes for God to restore ... (Acts 3:17,19-21)

The 'condition' was the people's repentance; "Repent.... that he may send the Christ.... to restore...." The word "repent" (*metanoeo*) means "a change of mind about something" (*NIV Theological Dictionary*) and in the context of its use here refers back to the disowning of Jesus by the "Men of Israel" and their killing of "the author of life". Peter, knowing that God had forgiven them (in answer to the Lord's prayer on the cross Luke 23:34) says to them, "I know that you acted in ignorance, as did your leaders", and he now calls upon them to 'have a change of mind'—"Repent, then, and turn to God, so that your sins may be wiped out ... and that he may send the Christ...—even Jesus" (vs.12-21). Israel were being offered a second chance to accept Jesus as the Christ (cp. John 20:30,31) and the Acts of the Apostles is the record of that act of grace.

So then, the "hope" of these early believers was that the "kingdom" would be restored to Israel at the return of the Lord to the Mount of Olives, "in the same way you have seen him go". The unfulfilled Old Testament prophecies concerning Israel would be fulfilled and (what we today call "the Millennium") would be set up on earth. This "hope" prevailed throughout the period of the Acts of the Apostles. It was this "hope" that the disciples asked about just before the Lord's ascension, "Lord, are you at this time going to *restore* the kingdom to Israel"? (Acts 1:6, A.D.33) and it was the "hope" Paul spoke of to the Jewish leaders in Rome, "It is because of the *hope* of Israel that I am bound with this chain". This hope he had described some two years earlier to king Agrippa as, "the promise our twelve tribes are hoping to see fulfilled" (Acts 28:20; 26:7 A.D. 61).

## Pentecost and After

The nucleus of believers at Pentecost, part of an increasing company who were eventually to be called "Christians", were the twelve disciples of Christ. (Their number was made up from eleven to twelve for a reason that had a great deal to do with their "hope"; Acts 1:21-26 and see Matthew 19:28.) There were also a number of women and other brethren, making a total compliment of "about a hundred and twenty" persons (vs. 13-15). That number was shortly increased by 3000 and later to about 5000 (Acts 2:41; 4:4). The message they believed and acted upon was that preached by Peter, John and the other apostles, and two examples of that message are given in Acts 2:14-40 and 3:12-26. On both of those occasions he called upon his own people ("Men of Israel ... brothers … heirs of the prophets" (2:22,36; 3:17,25) to "repent" and in both cases linked what was happening to Old Testament prophecies.

These early believers were Jews and proselytes (converts to Judaism) who had gathered at Jerusalem for the feast of Pentecost from many parts of the known world (Acts 2:5-11; 6:5). This company of Jews and proselytes did not separate themselves from their unbelieving Jewish brethren, but continued to go to the Jerusalem Temple and observe the Law of Moses, even circumcising their male children (Acts 2:46; 3:1; 5:42; 16:1-3; cp. 21:20-24) and their teaching and way of life came to be called "the Way" (9:2; 19:9,23 etc). They were looked upon as another "sect" within Judaism, "the Nazarene sect" (Acts 24:5): The Sadducees and the Pharisees are also called "sects" (same Greek word) in Acts (5:17; 15:5 *KJV*).

They practised a form of true communism, having "everything in common" and, "selling their possessions and goods", "they gave to anyone as he had need" (Acts 2:44,45; 4:32). F.F. Bruce has suggested the possibility that they formed their own synagogue, "the synagogue of the Nazarenes". Since the purpose of a synagogue was for the reading and exposition of the Law, it would be natural for them to come together to hear the Old Testament expounded by the apostles in the light of the revelation that Jesus of Nazareth, now risen from the dead, was the long awaited Christ.

Although the practice of having all things "common" is not mentioned again after Acts 4:32, and with the persecution that arose especially after the martyrdom of Stephen (Acts 7), many were scattered abroad from Jerusalem. However, "Christian" assemblies continued to look after poorer brethren as a priority (Acts 24:17; Galatians 2:10; Romans 15:25,26). The New Testament doesn't specifically say that other "Christian" assemblies, formed after the scattering of the early believers from Jerusalem, shared "the common property", but the practice was by no means unknown even prior to

Pentecost. For example, the Jewish sect, known as the Essenes, living in various communities throughout Palestine (circa 150 BC-AD 70) held their goods in common. Later, within Christendom, monastic sects arose in which monks and nuns lived in such communities and this still happens today. But we find no direct command to share "the common property" anywhere in the New Testament and the practice seems to have been purely voluntary (cp. Acts 5:4) and may have only lasted for a short time.

But there is another reason why this 'communal' spirit occupied these early believers—the "hope" of the expectation of the early return of the Christ and the consequent "restoration" of "everything … promised long ago through his holy prophets" (Acts 3:20,21). This "hope of Israel", involving the "twelve tribes" spoken about in the Prophets, included the restoration of the Land of Promise to Israel, allocated to those tribes and set out in specific terms in Ezekiel 47:13-48:29. And set over those twelve tribes the Lord had promised to the twelve apostles that, "at the renewal of all things, when the Son of Man sits on his glorious throne, *you who have followed me will also sit on twelve thrones, judging the twelve tribes of Israel"* (Matthew 19:28). It was for this reason that it was so important to make up their number to twelve after the defection of Judas Iscariot (Acts 1:15-26).

But Christ did not return during the lifetime of those early believers who were prepared to give up so much and suffer so much for Him, and who looked for His imminent coming. Even today we still await that coming. A few years after the end of the period covered by the Acts of the Apostles, Jerusalem was destroyed and its temple burned by Titus, and many Jews were taken captive to Rome (A.D. 70). Jerusalem, a continuing centre of authority throughout the Acts period (1:4; 8:1; 15:1,2; 21:17) could no longer be looked upon in that way. So what had gone wrong —the answer, as it had so often been in Israel's past, lay in *the human factor.*

John the Baptist had preached to Israel, "Repent, for the kingdom of heaven is near" and the Lord had reiterated that call (Matthew 3:1,2; 4:17).

After the resurrection Peter continued the call to "repentance" to his brethren (Acts 2:38; 3:19). It was used in the context of the presence (or promised presence) of the Lord (the King) and the nearness of the setting up of "the kingdom of heaven" (or as *Moffatt* translates, "the *reign* of heaven") on earth. God was calling The Nation to "repentance", a *response* necessary for these things to come to pass. However, *the human factor* was involved and their non-repentance led to the delay (in human terms) of the return of Christ and the setting up of that kingdom.

We must not however, get the idea that 'the human factor' in any way implies that God is either taken by surprise, or that He has to initiate a contingency plan when man disobeys Him. He knows the end from the beginning (Isaiah 46:9,10) and is not limited to seeing things in a linear plane as we are. Past, present and future are all one to Him, since he sees the whole scenario from beginning to end. Because of His foreknowledge he can predestine (Romans 8:29: cp. Acts 2:23; 1 Peter 1:2). Nevertheless, we cannot discount that 'the human factor' has played a part in the working out of His purposes, because He is not looking for 'lip service' from man, but some return of the love He has lavished upon us. His complaint to Israel was, "These people honour me with their lips, but their hearts are far from me" (Isaiah 29:13; Matthew 15:8).

## The Return of Christ

In Acts chapter 1, the return of Christ is referred to immediately after His ascension. Gathered together on the Mount of Olives, the apostles see Jesus, "taken up before their very eyes, and a cloud hid him from their sight". As they looked intently up into the sky as He was going, "two men dressed in white stood beside them" and said:

> "Men of Galilee … Why do you stand here looking into the sky? This same Jesus, who has been taken from you into heaven, *will come back in the same way* you have seen him go into heaven." (Acts 1:9-12)

This should not have taken them by surprise, and perhaps I am wrong in even hinting that it might have done, for the return of Christ to the Mount of Olives was part of Old Testament prophecy still awaiting fulfilment, and just as He ascended through the clouds, so He would come back "in the same way":

> A day of the LORD is coming … on that day his feet will stand on the Mount of Olives … One like a son of man, coming with the clouds of heaven. (Zechariah 14:1-4; Daniel 7:13; see also Matthew 24:30; Revelation 1:7)

Putting ourselves in the place of these men, we will surely conclude that they expected this promise to be fulfilled shortly—their Lord was coming back to them, within their own lifetime. They could never have imagined that this promise would still await fulfilment nearly 2000 years later. In fact, the hope of Christ's early return, with its promise of restoration promised through the prophets, remained strong throughout the period covered by the Acts of the Apostles.

Epistles written during this period make it clear that the writers believed that they were living in days that were expected to immediately precede that coming, e.g. Romans 13:11,12; 1 Corinthians 10:11; Hebrews 10:25; James 5:7-9; 1 Peter 4:7; 1 John 2:18, and Paul even wrote to the Thessalonians concerning "we *who are still alive*, who are left till the coming of the Lord" as though he expected to be one of them (1 Thessalonians 4:15; see also 1 Corinthians 15:51,52).

I know that Christians throughout the ages have looked for the Lord's second coming, and some have even claimed to know the date, only to be proved wrong. A few have sold their possessions in the light of their conviction, and gathered on some hill or mountain to await His coming, only to be disappointed. The belief that he would return "to judge the living and the dead" was built into the Creeds that were formulated during the early centuries of Christendom, and affirmed every Sunday by worshippers. But while many Christians believe that He could return "any minute", I don't think it is unfair to say that the average "Christian" today does not live in the conscious anticipation of this.

But this was not true of those who stood on the Mount of Olives and heard the Old Testament promise repeated by the "men dressed in white", even though they had been warned that they could not know "the times or dates the Father has set by his own authority". And their consequent words and actions were completely in line with their expectation. This expectation, and the hope that at His return they would receive their inheritance (by tribe) in The Promised Land (Ezekiel 47,48) may have sparked off their readiness to have all things "common". Had not Peter promised on the basis of their repentance, not only that their sins would be "wiped out", but that:

> Times of refreshing may come from the Lord, and that *he may send the Christ*, who has been appointed for you—*even Jesus*. He must remain in heaven until the time comes for God to *restore everything, as he*

*promised long ago through his holy prophets.* (Acts 3:18-21)

But Christ did not return *at that time*, and the promised "restoration" *at that time,* never took place: The reason being that Israel never had 'a change of mind' towards Jesus of Nazareth, never responded to His disciples' call to repent; only a "remnant" responded (Romans 11:1-7,25,26).

The Acts of the Apostles is a commentary on that failure. I emphasise the words, "at that time", because I am convinced that, in spite of their rejection of Christ as a nation, Israel will one day accept Him and the unfulfilled, irrevocable promises of the Old Testament will be fulfilled at His second coming. That is still future to us today but that is another subject and outside the scope of this booklet; (see Appendix 2 *The Future Hope of Israel*).

As the Acts period wore on, the hope of the return of Christ and the promised restoration may have begun to fade in the minds of some believers, but that "hope" remained sure and certain as far as men like Paul were concerned. Appearing before Agrippa towards the end of the Acts period (A.D.60) he said to the king:

> It is because of my hope in what God has promised our fathers that I am on trial today. This is *the promise our twelve tribes are hoping to see fulfilled* as they earnestly serve God day and night. (Acts 26:6,7)

He went on to say that he said "nothing beyond what Moses and the prophets said would happen" (v.22). And later in Acts 28:20 (A.D. 61) he still maintains, to the leaders of the Jews, that "the hope of Israel" is relevant to the time. That "hope" was 'live' from the beginning to the end of the Acts period. Everything that is written in the Acts and the epistles that belong to that period has to be understood in the light of that hope. So where, at this time, do the Gentiles come in? What was their hope and status? What did Gentile "Christians" hope for?

# The Inclusion of the Gentiles

Luke's record in Acts is set out very carefully as he tells of the progress of the early preaching of the word; especially with respect to when the Gentiles were first called. And he makes it clear that the salvation of the Gentiles *at that time* came as a surprise to Jewish believers. Of course, Gentiles who were converts to Judaism were included from the very beginning (Acts 2:11; 6:5), but it required a vision from the Lord to get Peter to even visit a godly Gentile and refer to "the message God sent to the People of Israel, telling the good news of peace through Jesus Christ"(Acts 10:9-16,28; 10:34-36).

Now we can take the line that, even though Peter was a believer, he was still at root a bigoted Jew. Or, more realistically, we can accept that a change was taking place in the Lord's dealings with Israel, a change that, *at that time*, came as a surprise even to believing Jews. That Israel was to be used to bring blessing to the Gentile nations was never in any doubt. This was written in the

Old Testament and still acknowledged in the New (Genesis 12:1-3; Acts 13:46,47 quoting Isaiah 49:6). But should Gentiles be approached *before* Israel was saved and ready to fulfil their place in God's purpose? Jewish believers could not contemplate this. So why was this change introduced?

Paul explains the whole position at length in Romans chapters 9-11 and these should be read to get the full impact of Paul's arguments there. However, look at just five verses (11:1,11-14) that give one reason for this apparent change in God's dealings with Israel. Referring to the fact that "not all the Israelites accepted the good news" (10:16) he writes:

> I ask then: Did God reject his people? By no means! ... Did they (Israel) stumble so as to fall beyond recovery? Not at all! Rather, because of their transgression, *salvation has come to the Gentiles to make Israel envious* ... I am talking to you Gentiles. Inasmuch as I am the apostle to the Gentiles, *I make much of my ministry in*

*the hope that I may somehow arouse my own people to envy and save some of them.*

We must not of course read this as though the *only* reason God turned to the Gentiles *at that time* was to use them as a kind of prod, to try and wake up the Jews by making them envious of the Gentiles. This might give the impression that Gentiles were inferior to Jews. But as Peter said at the conversion of the gentile Cornelius, "I now realise how true it is that God *does not show favouritism* but accepts men from every nation who fear him and do what is right" (Acts 10:34,35; see also Romans 10:12; Galatians 3:28).

Here we have another case of "times and dates" being set by the Father's authority (Acts 1:7) and it introduces one of those mysteries that we may never fathom in the way God works; "because of their (Israel's) transgression, salvation has come to the Gentiles … As far as the gospel is concerned, they are enemies on your (you Gentiles) account; but as far as election is concerned, they are loved on account of the patriarchs, for God's gifts and his call are irrevocable" (Romans 11:11,28,29). The failure of Israel leads to the salvation of the Gentiles, but not so that Israel are finally rejected, for God's gifts and call are irrevocable, they cannot be revoked. The day will come when "all Israel will be saved" (11:26). No wonder at the end of this difficult chapter Paul breaks out into a doxology, "Oh, the depth of the riches of the wisdom and knowledge of God! How unsearchable his judgements, and his paths beyond tracing out!" (v. 33).

## Peter's Keys

The (false) claim by the Popes to derive divine authority from Peter through 'Apostolic Succession', should not fudge the very real truth that the Lord gave to Peter an authority that was given to none of the other Apostles—"The keys of the kingdom of heaven":

> You are Peter, and on this rock I will build my church, and the gates of Hades will not

overcome it. *I will give you the keys of the kingdom of heaven*; whatever you bind on earth will be bound in heaven, and whatever you loose on earth will be loosed in heaven. (Matthew 16:18,19)

Peter was given "the keys of *the kingdom of heaven*", the reign of heaven over the earth, **not** the "kingdom of God" as a whole. Those keys were limited to the earthly hope of Israel and that "church" which was being called out during the Gospel and Acts period. Those keys have nothing to do with the church which is The Body of Christ revealed after the Acts period in Ephesians and Colossians and whose hope lies in "the heavenly realms" (Ephesians 1:3).

Peter used those keys on the day of Pentecost to his own people (Acts 2:14-39). While all the apostles there were filled by the Holy Spirit and declared "the wonders of God" in other tongues (vs. 4,6,11), it was **Peter** who "stood up with the Eleven, raised **his voice** and addressed the crowd: Fellow Jews and all of you who live in Jerusalem" (v.14).

Peter used those keys again on his visit to the godly Gentile, Cornelius (Acts 10:34-44) an action that was later reflected in Paul and Barnabas, how "God ... had *opened the door* of faith to the Gentiles" (Acts 14:27). As Peter testified, speaking to the apostles and elders in Jerusalem, "God made a choice among you that *the Gentiles might hear from my lips* the message of the gospel and believe" (Acts 15:6,7). Paul may have been called by the Lord to minister especially to the Gentiles (Acts 9:15; Galatians 2:7-9) but it was Peter who was chosen to first take the message of the gospel to them—to use the keys to open "the kingdom of heaven" to them.

This development was a surprise to some of the Jews *at that time*, and when Peter returned to Jerusalem he was challenged by "the circumcised believers" there about his visit to Cornelius, but after he related the circumstances, "They had no further objections and praised God, saying, 'So, then, God has granted even the Gentiles repentance unto life'" (Acts 11:1-18).

Gentile "Christians" called out "*at that time*" were to "share" in the salvation that was offered to Israel. Paul explains this at some length in Romans chapters 9-11 where he uses the figure of an Olive tree (Israel) that has some of its branches (Jews) broken off and branches taken from a wild Olive (Gentiles) grafted in "contrary to nature" (11:11-24). It was this inclusion of the Gentiles *at that time*, a development that was "contrary to nature", that surprised Peter and others of his race.

I cannot emphasise too much that Romans chapters 9-11 should be read to get the full impact of Paul's arguments there[2], giving the status of the Gentile Christian *at that time*. The development of the purpose of God in which the

---

[2] For a fuller treatment of this see *God's Grand Design* by Charles Ozanne, and also *Romans: Background and Introduction* by Brian Sherring: both published by The Open Bible Trust.

Gentiles *now*, *at that time*, were being called to salvation (described by Paul in these chapters) sums up the position of the Gentiles during the period covered by The Acts of the Apostles. And their 'hope' was intimately bound up with that of Israel, since they were "grafted in among the 'branches' (of Israel) and shared in the nourishing sap from the olive root" (Romans 11:17).

It is difficult to believe that this position still obtains today, and it is evident that the Lord's 'patience' eventually ran out with this "disobedient and obstinate people" (Romans 10:21). They closed their eyes and they shut their ears to the word of truth (Acts 28:26,27); they continued to reject Jesus as the Christ – *the human factor cut in* – and their hope, "the hope of Israel", went into abeyance. Paul, the apostle to the Gentiles, was entrusted to announce to the Jewish leaders in Rome:

> Therefore, I want you to know that God's salvation has been sent to the Gentiles, and they will listen. (Acts 28:28)

*Christians: Their Message and their Witness* 58

When Peter went to the godly Gentile Cornelius he spoke of the word of salvation as, "the message God *sent to the people of Israel*, telling the good news of peace through Jesus Christ" (Acts 10:36); now Paul tells the Jews that God has *sent God's salvation* to the Gentiles.

The full implications of this statement cannot be understood from these words alone. We need to study those epistles Paul wrote *after* that event, comparing them with what was written before, to understand the position of the Christian today.

## The Christian Hope Today

A believing Gentile living during the period covered by the Acts of the Apostles, would be faced with the following statements showing that the Jew had priority of position in the purpose of God *at that time*.

> We had to speak the word of God *to you (Jews) first*. (Acts 13:46)

*Christians: Their Message and their Witness* 59

The gospel … for the salvation of everyone who believes: *first for the Jew*, then for the Gentile. (Romans 1:16)

What *advantage*, then, is there *in being a Jew … Much in every way*! First of all, they have been entrusted with the very words of God. (Romans 3:1,2)

The people of *Israel. Theirs is* the adoption as sons; *theirs* the divine glory, the covenants, the receiving of the law, the temple worship and the promises. *Theirs are* the patriarchs, and *from them* is traced the human ancestry of Christ. (Romans 9:4,5)

You (Gentiles) were cut out of an olive tree that is wild by nature, and *contrary to nature* were grafted into a cultivated olive tree. (Romans 11:24)

None of this meant that Gentiles were inferior to the Jews, even *at that time*, or that their salvation was less secure than that of the Jew, but the

Gentile "Christian" did not stand in the same position in the purpose of God *at that time*, while He was pursuing His purpose through Israel in accordance with Old Testament covenants and promises. That is not the position today. Things have changed. In Paul's later epistles, especially Ephesians and Colossians, the position of the Gentile believer is seen to be exactly the same as that of the Jewish believer, not only as far as salvation is concerned, *but now also* as to his/her *status* before God.

The internal evidence in the New Testament Scriptures is that this change happened sometime after Acts 28:28 (A.D. 61), probably within the "two years" mentioned by Luke in verses 30,31. During this period the two epistles mentioned above were written and they set out the position and "hope" of the "Christian" today. They must be read through, perhaps many times, to appreciate how different the Christian 'hope' is today. I give just a few pointers, but I trust that readers will want to verify them for themselves and make them their own.

Paul opens Ephesians by speaking of "spiritual blessings" in "heavenly realms" (1:3,20). He says to the Ephesian "saints", "God raised us up with Christ and seated us with him in the heavenly realms in Christ Jesus" (2:6). It is difficult to square this with the earthly hope resident in "the promise our twelve tribes are hoping to see fulfilled" (Acts 26:7). In fact Paul, in Ephesians 1:18 actually prays for the Ephesians, "that the eyes of your heart may be enlightened *in order that you may know the hope to which he has called you*".

They needed to be "enlightened" as to what that "hope" was. Surely these Ephesians knew their hope; did not Paul spend two years and three months, the longest stay in any one missionary location in Ephesus (Acts 19)? And later, when he said farewell to the Ephesian elders on his way to Rome he declared, "I have not shunned to declare unto you *all the counsel of God*" (Acts 20:27 A.D.58). Did that not include what their "hope" was? So why then is he praying for them in his letter to the Ephesians some three years later (A.D. 61)?

The answer lies in the fact that following the Lord's judgement pronounced to the Jewish leaders at Rome (Acts 28:26,27), the "hope" of the Acts period, "the hope of Israel" (28:20) went into abeyance and the Lord turned to the Gentiles through Paul, and revealed another "hope" that had nothing to do with the covenants and promises made with Israel. Hence the Ephesians needed to be "enlightened" as to what it was. It is revealed to them (and us) in two of the letters Paul wrote during his two years in Roman confinement (Acts 28:30,31 A.D. 61)— Ephesians and Colossians.

In Acts Gentiles were "grafted in" among the branches of Israel in the Olive tree of Romans 11, now they are "heirs together with Israel" in the one body (3:6). In Acts, Paul confines his message to "saying nothing beyond what the prophets and Moses said would happen" (26:22) but in both Ephesians and Colossians he speaks of "the mystery … not made known to men in other generations *as it has now been revealed.*" This mystery, or secret, had just been revealed for previously it had been "kept hidden for ages and generations, *but now disclosed* to the saints" (Ephesians 3:3-5; Colossians 1:26).

Put briefly, God is today running an administration under which Jew and Gentile 'hope' is no longer "the hope of Israel" and linked to promises made to them in the Old Testament, but points us to the very right hand of God, where we are seen seated with Christ in the heavenlies. Our means of salvation rest, as it always has in any dispensation of God, on the person and work of Christ.

But we must leave Israel's hope to a future day, when "the times or dates the Father has set by his own authority" will come to pass, and He will reinstate that hope and their Messiah will return to them to set up His kingdom on earth. In the meantime our priority is to seek to understand as much as the Lord has revealed of our heavenly hope and to witness accordingly as "Christians".

# Chapter 3: Christian Witness

Christian witness is initially a witness to a Person, to **the Lord Jesus Christ**. This has never changed, nor should it. Christians today accept the full implications of this 'name', unlike the Jews on the Day of Pentecost who had to be convinced with the words, "God has made this **Jesus**, whom you crucified, **both Lord and Christ**" (Acts 2:36). This assertion was based on the fact of the resurrection of Christ—"God has raised this Jesus to life, and we are all *witnesses* of the fact" (v.32). Christian witness is a witness to a *living* Christ.

Secondly, and issuing from this belief, is a witness to Him by *a way of life*. The verb 'to witness' (Greek *martureo*) is first translated in the Acts of the Apostles (*KJV*) as "of honest report" and "of good report" (6:3; 10:22); these men were *attested to* by others; their way of life was their witness. A person's honest or good way of life need not of course be based upon belief in Christ and I will return to this later in the context of witness. Here I am concerned with a way of life, a witness that proceeds from trust in Christ.

## Christian Witness: Parameters

It is fairly obvious that however hard we try we cannot force others to accept what we believe to be the truth. We can present our case, even (in our own opinion) prove our point, but in the final analysis it is down to the hearer's willingness or ability to accept or reject it. Put in terms of an ancient proverb, "you can take a horse to the water, but you can't make it drink". So when we begin to think about our own Christian witness, we must be aware of its parameters, its limitations and its place in the purpose of God.

These thoughts also suggest questions such as, "If we cannot make others believe in Jesus Christ as their Saviour, what is the point of trying?" We may also begin to think that our witness is of small importance in the great purpose of God;

those who are going to believe, will believe and vice versa. He doesn't need us anyway, does He? I need hardly say this view, bordering on extreme Calvinism, is neither logical nor scriptural and it is soul destroying.

As a young Christian I was instilled by older Christians with the necessity of preaching the Gospel to the unsaved. Very commendable you might say, but this was put to me in such a way so as to imply that if I didn't, others would be lost and would perish in their sins. In other words their salvation rested on my faithfulness. Even at the time, when I was largely unversed in the Scriptures, I felt that this was a burden that neither I, nor anyone else could bear. Could I really be held responsible for another's salvation?

With more knowledge of the Bible's teaching, I came to realise that there was in fact no scriptural promise that even if I faithfully presented to the unbeliever their need of a Saviour, they would necessarily become believers. I could see that even Paul, who from the Old Testament

Scriptures could "prove" that Jesus is the Christ to those who were actually looking for Him and believed those Scriptures, *could not guarantee* that his listeners would believe and accept Jesus as the Christ. In fact they quite often didn't (Acts 9:22,23; 17:1-4; 18:5,6,28). I also came to realise that Christian witness was not confined to witnessing to unbelievers, but was much wider in its scope, including not only believers but also heavenly beings (more of this later).

So, with the above thoughts in mind, what is the purpose and object of Christian witness to unbelievers? Is it just a "feel good" factor for the Christian, or does it play an important part in the outworking of God's purpose for mankind? What are its parameters? To answer this we need to see it in the context of God's witness to mankind in all its manifestations as defined by the Scriptures.

## Christian Witness in Context

Christian witness is just one of a number of ways in which God himself speaks or witnesses to man. He has spoken, both in the past and the present by means of the earthly and heavenly creation, the conscience, visions and dreams, covenants, the Scriptures and finally through His Son. (See *Search* vols.120, 121 for articles on this subject). To these we can add that He also uses mankind as a channel and witness to convey His truths; witnesses to the truth of His Word, by word and life.

As we have observed there is no guarantee that any will respond to our witness, but this is true of every form of "witness" that God has given to man. The heavens declare the glory of God and the firmament shows His handiwork (Psalm 19), but many have no room for Him as the Creator—this "witness" can fall on deaf ears: "The fool says in his heart, 'There is no God'" (Psalm 14:1; 53:1).

The Scriptures witness to Him, but how many believe them to be the Word of God? When the Lord spoke to His disciples concerning events that would precede His second coming He said, "this gospel of the kingdom shall be preached in all the world *for a witness* to all nations; and then shall the end come" (Matthew 24:14 *KJV*), but He also said, "When the Son of Man comes, *will he find faith on the earth?*" (Luke 18:8). The Lord never guaranteed that many would respond to the Gospel as a result of the witness of believers. So, coming back to the negative thoughts that Christian witness is a waste of time, that there is no point in it and that our witness as an individual is of small importance in the great purpose of God, what shall we say?

Well, firstly, is it not a privilege that we have been called to be part of God's witness to others by declaring His truths and showing it in the lives we lead? And if God has shown such patience in His dealings with man, in spite of apparently little response, who are we to give up because we see little or nothing for our efforts to witness to Christ? Christian witness is important, it is part of that great "witness" to Him and His purpose, however small it may seem in our own eyes and however little the response may appear to be. It is in this context that Christian witness must be seen. There is also another side to this witness.

In what I have written so far, I may have given the impression that the Christian, in witnessing to his or her faith, stands alone, and that whether or not others respond to that witness is entirely dependent upon that Christian's efforts. This, however, is not the case.

Apart from the fact that we work together with other believers (see 1 Corinthians 3:6-9), the Lord Himself works with us. The Lord never left His first disciples to their own devices, but promised in the context of the ministry He committed to them, "Lo, *I am with you always, even to the end of the age*" (Matthew 28:19,20 lit). *Moffatt's* version translates this as, "all the time I will be with you". They were given the assurance that they were never alone, the Lord would work with them, as Mark noted in his Gospel, "The disciples went out and preached everywhere, *and the Lord worked with them*" (16:20).

John, in his Gospel, interprets this 'presence' of the Lord when he records the Lord's own words to His disciples: "I will ask the Father, and he will give you another Counsellor *to be with you for ever* (lit. for the age)—the Spirit of truth … I will not leave you as orphans; *I will come to you*" (14:15-18). The Lord was 'present' with His disciples through the Holy Spirit, another Counsellor, and so "worked with them" (cp. Luke 24:47-49). We may not be Apostles, committed to a worldwide 'discipling' of the nations, but in our own small way the same Lord has not left us alone—He is with us in our witness to Him. Do we need more encouragement than this?

## Christian Witness: Two Aspects

Christian witness in Scripture is basically seen under two heads: Personal and Corporate.

**Personal witness:** The witness of an individual to Christ, and the salvation that is offered through Him and His sacrifice. It involves not only telling unbelievers about their need of a Saviour and urging their acceptance of Him, but is also to believers, where the more mature can help others to come to a better knowledge of Him and His purpose. In both cases "witness" is not confined to conversation only, but involves also the life lived. Within this group there are those who have been called out for special responsibility; Prophets, Apostles etc, but we are all involved in individual witness, one way or another. This individual witness is part of:

**Corporate witness:** The witness of a 'body' of people who have been drawn together into (e.g.) a church or a nation. The two examples in Scripture are

**a) Israel:** The witness of Israel as a nation to the other nations of the earth. They were called out to be prepared for their place in world blessing and to be God's witnesses to His truths on earth—"a light for the Gentiles" (Acts 13:46,47). Only when they accept Jesus as their Messiah, at His second coming, will they be fitted for this task that had its beginnings during the Acts period (cp. Matthew 28:19; Acts 1:8). The witness of Israel to the nations of the earth is beyond the remit of this booklet; it is a subject by itself. That witness stands in abeyance at the present time.

**b) The Body of Christ:** The witness of The Church, the Body of Christ that reveals to principalities and powers in the heavenly realms the manifold wisdom of God (Ephesians 3:10,11). The witness of the individual Christian today within the Church, the Body of Christ, is part of the corporate witness of the whole 'body' before Principalities and Powers in the heavenly realms.

## Witness to Principalities and Powers

In an epistle in which Paul claims to have received an administration from God that particularly involves the Gentiles, he writes (Ephesians 3:8-11 *KJV*):

> To me (Paul).... is this grace given, that I should preach among the Gentiles the unsearchable riches of Christ; and to make

all men see what is the fellowship (dispensation or stewardship) of the mystery, which from the beginning of the world has been hid in God….**to the intent that now to the principalities and powers in heavenly places might be known by (means of) the church** the manifold wisdom of God, according to the eternal purpose which he purposed in Christ Jesus our Lord.

God's choice of a Body of Christians to be associated with Christ far above all in the heavenly realms (2:6) has, as one of its objects, a *witness* to spiritual beings of "the manifold wisdom of God". Here, the *fellowship* (literally, stewardship) of the mystery, which had been hidden from the ages in God and which involves the Gentiles, is made known. The word "fellowship" is important here, for that is just what is required for a 'body' of people to function smoothly as a corporate 'body'. So we should ask, *as a Body of Christians*, part of God's purpose for the heavenly realms, how do we stand? Personal witness is one thing, but we are actually called *as a Body* to "the *fellowship* of the mystery", vertically a fellowship with Christ, but horizontally fellowship with others.

One of the criticisms levelled against Christians generally is that they are divided amongst themselves, as evidenced by the numerous sects and denominations that exist. But within the Body of Christ a unity has already been made, "the unity of the Spirit", which we are urged to "keep ... through (*en* in) the bond of peace". This is neither easy nor happens automatically, hence Paul urges us to "make every effort" to keep it (Ephesians 4:3). The word translated "make every effort" here is the Greek *spoudazo*, used of Paul's *eagerness* to "remember the poor" (Galatians 2:10) and of the *diligence* needed (*NIV* "do your best") to present oneself as an approved workman "who does not need to be ashamed and who correctly handles the word of truth" (2 Timothy 2:15). The implication is that it may not always be possible to keep "the unity of the Spirit", as it very much depends on each member (part) of that Body:

*Christians: Their Message and their Witness* 76

Speaking truth in love we may grow into Him, who is the Head, the Christ … of whom all the body being fitted together and compacted together through every ligature of assistance **according to (the) working in measure of each one part**, producing the growth of the body to the building up of itself in love. (Ephesians 4:15,16 lit.)

This passage belongs to the practical section of Ephesians and began with the exhortation, "I urge you to live a life worthy of the calling you have received" (4:1). It deals with the way the Body may 'grow' *in a practical sense*. That Body may be effectively "seated with Christ in the heavenlies" but it also has a *witness* down here on earth, a witness that is going to depend (corporately) on the effectiveness of "each one part", an effectiveness and growth that is grounded in love: "Speaking truth *in love* we may grow"; "building up itself *in love*".

Literature published by *The Open Bible Trust* must be in accordance with its evangelical, fundamental and dispensational basis. Beyond these its authors are free to express their own personal beliefs providing their aim is to further the object of the Trust to the glory of the Lord. Christians are almost bound to hold differences of opinion on some subjects, but this should not lead to withdrawal from fellowship with other members of the Body of Christ. The growth of this Body, in practical terms, depends on "the working in measure of each one part"; the Greek is very forceful, not 'every' but "of each one part". All are needed for this corporate witness to "the rulers and authorities in the heavenly realms". "There is one body," not many (Ephesians 4:4).

It is a humbling thought that Christians in the Church, the Body of Christ, have been chosen not only to sit in the heavenly realms, but, as a 'body', used by God to reveal His manifold wisdom to heavenly beings. The marvel of it is that the individual is not lost sight of in the vastness of this purpose, but his or her 'witness' contributes to the building up of this body in love, "as each part does its work" (Ephesians 4:16).

## Witness and Judgement

We observed that however faithfully we witness to Christ in both word and deed, there is no guarantee it will lead to anyone accepting Christ or have any noticeable effect on them. I say 'noticeable', because we may never know in this life just what effect our witness, poor though it is, has had on those we come into contact with. This thought should at least give us some comfort when it sometimes seems that we are wasting our time.

There is another aspect of witness however, somewhat disturbing maybe, that the Scriptures touch upon—its relationship to judgement. When the Lord sent out the twelve disciples to go from village to village preaching repentance, He said to them, "If any place will not welcome you or listen to you, shake the dust off your feet when you leave, *as a testimony (witness) against them*"

(Mark 6:11) and in Matthew's account (10:11-15) this is expanded when the Lord adds, "I tell you the truth, it will be more bearable for Sodom and Gomorrah *on the day of judgement* than for that town".

We must of course see these passages in context, for we know that the 'witness' of the Lord and His disciples was often accompanied by miracles (cp. Matthew 11:23,24 lit. 'acts of power') and we are surely under no illusion that our witness does not measure up to theirs, even apart from miracles. But it seems that God's judgement of all men will be on the basis of their response to the light they are given, and this will determine how responsible they will be held to be on the day of judgement. This much can be seen in the passages quoted above concerning a judgement that is "more bearable" because of response to things seen (miracles in this case). It can also be felt in the words, "From everyone who has been given much, much will be demanded; and from the one who has been entrusted with much, much more will be asked" (Luke 12:48). (For a fuller exposition of this principle see *Search* No. 113, 'Light and Responsibility'.)

These two factors, light and responsibility, in God's judgement are like the two sides of a pair of scales; balancing each other out and producing perfect justice. So if the Lord calls us to witness before others to the 'light', i.e. "the true light that gives light to every man" who came into the world (John 1:9), whether by word or life, then it may be that those who hear or observe us may be judged on their response *to our witness*, a humbling thought and a great responsibility.

## Witness: The Ultimate Price

Readers will probably be aware that the word 'witness' is a translation of the Greek *martur* that comes into English as 'martyr', and today it includes the idea that the ultimate price for faithful witness is death—martyrdom. The historian P. W. Gooch wrote, "the martyr dies as a testimony to the over-riding importance of some belief or commitment greater than life itself". Taken in the widest sense, martyrdom does not necessarily have to be associated with belief or witness to Christ, i.e. Christian witness. Some may have an over-riding belief in any person or cause and be so thoroughly committed to it, that they are prepared to pay the ultimate price of all – martyrdom. Hence there have been (and continue to be) religious, political and humanist martyrs. We are however, not concerned with these here, confining our subject to martyrdom that comes about through witness to the person of Christ.

Andrew Chandler in the book *The Terrible Alternative: Christian Martyrdom in the Twentieth Century* (Cassell 1998) wrote, "It is a rarely acknowledged truth that in the twentieth century more Christians have died for their faith than in any other age (including the great persecutions of the early centuries of the Church)". I found this a remarkable statement and difficult to believe, until I realised that most of the modern examples he was referring to were martyrs to Christian causes (civil rights, justice, peace etc) rather than direct witness to Christ

Himself. And strictly these, although we call them "Christian causes (or principles)" pre-date the earthly ministry of Christ, having their roots in the Old Testament (the laws God gave to Israel via Moses Exodus 20 etc). The Lord certainly added a dimension to those laws during His earthly ministry, as for example when he said, "You have heard that it was said to the people long ago … *But I tell you*" (Matthew 5:21,22 cp. also 22:34-40), but there have been those throughout the ages, who have stood for these "Christian principles" who knew nothing of Christ and His teaching, and died for their witness.

The martyrdoms of the early centuries were perhaps more clear-cut, in that they were direct witnesses to Christ, when even to be called a "Christian" might lead to death. In the comparatively comfortable Western society in which most readers of this booklet live, a Christian may be contradicted, reviled, even mildly persecuted, but to confess to being a Christian – to confess Christ – is unlikely to lead to martyrdom (not yet anyway).

Of the three occurrences of the word "Christian" in the New Testament, Peter's words in his first epistle (4:16) link the name to suffering: "If you suffer as a Christian, do not be ashamed, but praise God that you bear that name".

Not long after he wrote these words many were to suffer for that name, and many died as true witnesses to Christ, praising God as they paid the ultimate price of their trust in Him. Please God that, should we find ourselves in a similar position, we may find the strength to remain faithful, even unto death, to be true Christian witnesses. Paul wrote to Timothy, possibly just prior to his own martyrdom as a "Christian":

> Do not be ashamed to testify (*marturion*) about our Lord, or ashamed of me his prisoner. But join with me in suffering for the gospel, by the power of God, who has saved us and called us to a holy life—not because of anything we have done but because of his own purpose and grace. (2 Timothy 1:8,9)

## Count it all Joy

Thomas Jefferson in his original draft for the American Declaration of Independence considered "the pursuit of happiness" an inalienable right of man. The way the Christian message has at times been presented has led to anything but that, with the preaching of (e.g.) 'hell fire' producing fear and foreboding amongst Christians. But that is not what the Christian life should be about. 'Happiness' is largely defined in the world as dependent upon circumstances such as leisure activities and 'having fun'. For the Christian however, there is another word that expresses what life should be about and which is independent of circumstances—**joy**: 'Fun' is ephemeral; joy eternal: Fun is external; joy within the heart. James wrote:

> Consider it *pure joy*, my brothers, whenever you face trials of many kinds, **because you know** that the testing of your faith develops perseverance. Perseverance must finish its

work so that you may be mature and complete not lacking anything. (1:2-4)

Christian witness should be joyful, even under trial, and it can be so "because we know" the outcome—maturity and completeness. The experience of the trial or discipline may be unpleasant, painful even distressing at the time (Hebrews 12:11) but it may be *counted* as "pure joy" in anticipation of the outcome. Our great example, the Lord Jesus Christ, the One who perfects our faith, "endured the cross, scorning its shame"—"for the *joy* set before him" (Hebrews 12:2). In worldly terms, the Christian life may not be 'happy', but as long as we keep our eyes fixed on Christ Jesus we can even now experience that joy within, in some small way, that will in the fullness of time be part of the maturity and completeness of the goal of Christian witness.

# Appendix 1: Saint (hagios) in the New Testament

## Gospels and Acts

In the Gospels *hagios* is used mostly of "the *Holy* Spirit", occasionally of "the *holy* prophets, "the *holy* city", "the *holy* place" and "the *holy* angels". It is also used of Jesus, "the *Holy* (One)" who was in the womb of Mary (Luke 1:35), and in Mark 6:20 of John the Baptist a "*holy* (man)". In Matthew 27:50-53 (*KJV*) there is a rare reference to "many bodies of the *saints*" who "came out of the graves after (Christ's) resurrection, and went into the *holy* city, and appeared unto many" (v. 53). These "saints" are not identified, but since they were "many" and they went into Jerusalem, is it possible that they were (or at least included in) the "five hundred brethren" who saw Christ after His resurrection? (1 Corinthians 15:6).

In Acts *hagios,* just as in the Gospels, is mostly used of the *Holy* Spirit. Two out of the four places where it is rendered "saints" (*KJV*) however, refer to those believers who were persecuted by Saul. Ananias said to the Lord, "I have heard by many of this man (Saul), how much evil he has done to your *saints* in Jerusalem" (9:13, *KJV*), and later from the mouth of Paul himself, when recounting to Agrippa his persecution of believers before his conversion. "Many of the *saints* did I shut up in prison" (26:10, *KJV*). It is significant to note in this context, that although Saul was persecuting the "saints", the Lord considered that it was He, whom Saul was persecuting—"I am Jesus whom you persecute" (9:5, *KJV*). To persecute the saints, is to persecute the Lord himself.

## Peter, James, John, Jude and Revelation

To **Peter** the "saints" are "God's elect" and his particular emphasis is on the position of Israel in the purpose of God. Writing to his own people (the Jews) dispersed throughout Asia Minor, he reminds them that they are still, "a chosen people, a royal priesthood, a *holy* (*hagios*) nation, a people belonging to God" (1 Peter 2:9). He recalls the peculiar position of Israel as a nation before God, "a *holy* nation", and quoting from Leviticus 11:44, he writes "Be *holy*, because I (the Lord) am *holy*" (1 Peter 1:15,16).

To Peter the "saints" were Jewish believers, who, conscious of their calling of God promised in the Old Testament Scriptures, lived looking for the second coming of Christ and the setting up of God's kingdom on earth (Acts 1:6).

Peter, as he testified, was used by the Lord so "that the Gentiles might hear from my lips the message of the gospel and believe" (Acts 15:7) but it was Paul who was later to explain the significance of the Lord turning to the Gentiles at that time, in his illustration of the Olive tree into which Gentile branches were being grafted (Romans 11:11-24). And it is Paul who uses the word "saints" of both Jews and Gentiles.

**James**, who also wrote to the dispersion of the twelve tribes of Israel during the period covered by the Acts of the Apostles, does not use the word *hagios* once, but uses the cognate word *hagnizo* when he calls upon the "double minded" to "*purify* your hearts" (4:8). Writing to his own people, he addresses them as "my brothers": A *holy* nation and people do not necessarily live *holy* lives. The calling is by grace; the life lived the response of a *holy*, separated people.

**John** never uses the word *hagios* of believers in either his Gospel or Epistles, but does many times in Revelation. John is taken in spirit to the troubled times of the future day of the Lord spoken of by the prophets of old (1:10). He speaks of "the prayers of *the saints*", "patient endurance and faithfulness on the part of *the saints*", "the blood of *the saints*", "the righteous acts of *the saints*" and of the beast's "war against *the saints*" (5:8; 13:10; 17:6; 19:8; 13:1-8). After the thousand years during which Satan is bound, the final battle is fought when he is released and gathers the nations against "the camp of *the* *saints*…. the beloved city", and is destroyed (20:7-9 *KJV*). The usage by John, himself a Jew, of the word "nations" in this context, suggests that the "saints" referred to here are again Jewish believers (*the* Nation) at the time of the end, "the beloved city" being Jerusalem.

The book of Revelation is addressed to the seven churches (or assemblies) in Asia Minor. The reference in the letter to the Philadelpian assembly to "the *synagogue* of Satan" and those "who claim to be *Jews*" (3:9), together with the very many allusions to the Old Testament throughout the book, lead us to the conclusion that "the saints" here are also Jewish believers in the last days.

**Jude** uses *hagios* only once of humans, "the faith that was once for all entrusted to *the saints*" (v.3). Since that "faith" was initially deposited with the Jews, we cannot but believe that Jude, a Jew and brother of James, is referring to Jewish believers. His other references are to that *holy* faith, the *Holy* Spirit and to "the *holy* ones" (v.14

angels) prophesied by Enoch and associated with the coming of the Lord.

**Hebrews:** There is no agreement among scholars and commentators who wrote this epistle. I will not therefore include it under Paul's epistles. As the name implies it is very Jewish in both its subject and presentation. It too uses *hagios* of the *Holy* Spirit, but in three places uses it of "saints". In 3:1 (*KJV*)the writer addresses his readers as "*holy* brethren, partakers of the heavenly calling....". Later that "heavenly calling" is identified as a city prepared for them (11:16), surely the New Jerusalem of Revelation 21, so intimately associated there with Israel.

The Hebrews are commended for their ministering "to the *saints*" (6:10, *KJV*), reminiscent of Paul's intention to go to Jerusalem to "minister to the *saints*" there, taking a contribution for "the poor (Jewish) *saints*" (Romans 15:25-27). The writer's final salutation is to "them that have the rule over you, and all the *saints*".

In the New Testament books and epistles looked at so far, the "saints" are Jewish believers, and the use of the word to describe them so is but a continuation of its usage in the Old Testament. It described one who was called and set apart, and who should live godly and faithful lives. But now that separation was in response to the Gospel of Christ that called for repentance and trust in His name—"Save yourselves from this untoward generation" said Peter to his countrymen (Acts 2:40, *KJV*). When we come to Paul's epistles however, he uses the word also of believing Gentiles.

## Paul's Epistles

Paul's epistles occupy a large part of the New Testament, and so we are not surprised to find that references to the "saints" would appear more often in his writings than elsewhere. But (if we exclude Revelation, 13 occurrences) the word hardly appears anywhere apart from his epistles, and is used of believing Gentiles as well as believing Jews. A quick glance at any

Concordance (based on the original Greek word *hagios*) will demonstrate this in a moment. In spite of its use in the Old Testament and by the other Jewish writers (remember Paul was a Jew), he does not hesitate to address believing Gentiles as "saints". So what does he say about those "saints"?

## Called To Be Saints

In writing to the churches, Paul sometimes addresses believers as *"called (kletos) to be saints"* (Romans 1:7; 1 Corinthians 1:2, *KJV*). In Romans he has already described himself as "called (*kletos*) to be an apostle" (v.1) defining it as "having been *separated* to the gospel of God" (lit.). He was *called* to be an apostle; they were *called* to be saints. Behind this word is the suggestion of invitation, as its use in Matthew 22:14 demonstrates in the parable of the wedding feast, "Many are *invited (kletos)*, but few are chosen". Hence, whether called to be an apostle or a saint, there is no compulsion. Just as one can say no to a wedding invitation, or, having accepted, fail to honour the host by wearing the wedding garment provided, so those called are not forced to become saints or accept the cover of righteousness provided.

Those referred to by Paul were "among those who are called (*kletos*) to belong to Jesus Christ" (Romans 1:6) who had responded and hence could be named "saints", the separated ones. In the Corinthian passage they are described as, "sanctified in Christ Jesus and *called* (*kletos*) to be holy (saints *KJV*)". There are three aspects involved in being a saint that can be seen in Revelation 17:14, "They that are with him (i.e. the King of kings) are called (*kletos*), **and** chosen, **and** faithful" (*KJV*).

1) *Invited* to be a saint.
2) Having the *status* of a saint.
3) *Living* as a saint should.

# Appendix 2: The Future Hope for Israel

Various books are available from the Open Bible Trust that bear on the subject of the position of Israel in the purpose of God and the fact that He has not finished with them as a nation, but will take up His purpose with them, put into abeyance at the end of the Acts period. Here is a sample:

*Apocalypse: An Introduction to Revelation*: Brian Sherring

*Approaching the Bible* (esp. pages 253 to 266): Michael Penny

*Empires of the End-Time (Daniel)*: Charles Ozanne

*Introducing the Books of the Bible*: Brian Sherring

*Israel in the New Testament*: Michael Penny (editor)

*Paul's Three Ministries*: Michael Penny

*The Fourth Gentile Kingdom (Daniel and Revelation)*: Charles Ozanne

Further details of these books,
and the ones on other pages,
can be seen on **www.obt.org**

They can all be ordered from that
website and also from

The Open Bible Trust
Fordland Mount, Upper Basildon,
Reading, RG8 8LU, UK.

They are also all available as eBooks
from Amazon and Apple
and as KDP paperbacks from Amazon.

# Bibliography

The following main sources (in addition to those on the previous page) have been used or referred to:

**Bible Versions:**
*New International*
*King James*
*English Standard*
*Moffatt*
*Septuagint* (*LXX*) Greek Old Testament

**Books:**
Bettenson Henry: *Documents of the Christian Church* Oxford U.P. 1967 (paperback)
Bruce F.F. *The Acts of the Apostles*: The Tyndale Press 1965
Bullinger E.W: *The Witness of the Stars* (obtainable from OBT)
Chandler Andrew: *The Terrible Alternative*: *Christian Martyrdom in the 20th Century*: Cassell
John-Charles Peter: *Biblical Chronology* OBT
Josephus Flavius: *The Antiquities of the Jews*

(transl. W. Whiston) Thomas Nelson

Lightfoot J.B: *The Apostolic Fathers* Macmillan
    1926 (modern edition Baker 1989)

Shakespeare: *Romeo and Juliet*

Suetonius Gaius: *The Twelve Caesars* The Folio
    Society 1964

Tertullian: *Loeb Classical Library*

**Dictionaries:**

*Chambers Concise*: *Oxford English*: *NIV*
    *Theological*

**Magazines:**

*Search* Nos. 113,120,121

# About the author

Brian Sherring was born in Isleworth, Middlesex, England in 1932. Following a technical education, he took an engineering apprenticeship and worked for some years as a design draughtsman in agricultural engineering. He was one time Assistant Principal of The Chapel of the Opened Book in London and wrote for The Berean Expositor but now writes for *Search* magazine. He now lives with his wife in retirement in Surrey.

He has written a number of major books including:

The Ten Commandments
Messiah and His People
The Mystery of Ephesians
Romans: Background and Introduction

Details can be seen on **www.obt.org.uk**

Brian Sherring is a regular contributor to
*Search* magazine

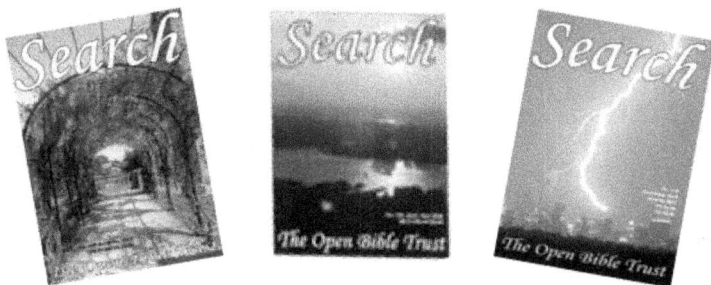

For a free sample of
The Open Bible Trust's magazine Search,
please email

**admin@obt.org.uk**

or visit

**www.obt.org.uk/search**

# Also by Brian Sherring

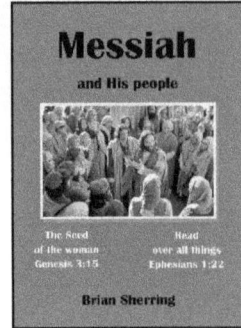

**Paul's Letter to the Romans**
Background & Introduction
Brian Sherring

**The Mystery of Ephesians**
The Mystery ...
as I have written briefly
(Ephesians 3:3)
Brian Sherring

**Messiah** and His people
The Seed of the woman Genesis 3:15
Head over all things Ephesians 1:22
Brian Sherring

## Paul's Letter to the Romans: Background & Introduction

This book sets Paul's letter to the Romans in the context of both the New Testament and his other letters. It gives the reader a good basis for a detailed study of the epistle.

It was written from Greece some three years before Paul arrived in Rome (Acts 20:2-3). This means that it was written *before* the judgement Paul pronounced upon the Jewish leaders in Rome (Acts 28:25-28). That is *before* Paul wrote Ephesians and Colossians in which new teachings are revealed about a heavenly calling,

*Christians: Their Message and their Witness* 102

about Gentile and Jewish equality, and about the abolishment of the Law of Moses. It is essential when reading Romans, not to read back into it such teaching as these, and the author does an excellent job of explaining Romans in its correct historical context.

## The Mystery of Ephesians

In Ephesians 3:3 Paul mentions a 'mystery', and states that he had written about it briefly, i.e. earlier in the letter. So ... What is this 'mystery'? ... Why have so few Christians heard about it? ... And why do some, who have heard about it, reject it? ... Even oppose it?

With great clarity Brian Sherring explains the Greek word   translated 'mystery' does not mean something 'mysterious' but refers to a 'secret', and this 'secret' is an important one. It relates to all mankind, and God had just revealed it to Paul and wanted Paul to make it known far and wide ... which is just what he did in writing Ephesians.

## Messiah and His People

In this book Brian Sherring takes the reader through the Bible and the unfolding portrait it paints of the Messiah, the Christ, the Redeemer.

He starts off in Genesis 3, where we learn of the seed of the woman who is to crush the serpent's head, and as we progress through time, slowly more and more is revealed about this One. He is to descend from Abraham and be of the house of David. He is to be born of a virgin and be born in Bethlehem.

He is to combine the offices of Prophet, Priest and King. From Ephesians 1 we learn that in the end He is to be head over all things and Philippians 2 states He is to have that Name which is above every name.

## Apocalypse
## An Introduction to
## Revelation

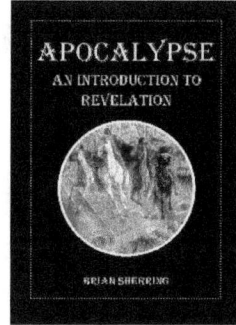

This is simply one of the best, if not *the* best, introduction to the Book of Revelation.

Revelation! A book that fascinates some Christians, but one that confuses others.

How can we start making sense of Revelation? Read this booklet. It will help you no end. It is not a detailed study which will bog you down. Rather it provides some keys that will unlock the last book of the Bible and enable Christians to begin to understand it and get it into perspective.

\*\*\*\*\*\*\*\*\*\*

These books can be ordered from
**www.obt.org.uk**

They are also all available as eBooks from
Amazon and Apple
and as KDP paperbacks from Amazon.

*Christians: Their Message and their Witness* 105

# About this book

## Christians!
### Their Message and their Witness

It is, perhaps, surprising, to find almost a total absence of the word "Christian" in the New Testament; there are only three references.

However, the word is much used today both in the church and in secular society. One dictionary defines "Christian" as "a decent, respectable person" (*Chambers Concise*). However, we need to remind ourselves that the first six letters of the word spell Christ", and that without Him and His sacrifice for our sins, the word is meaningless.

In this booklet the author looks at the origin and meaning of the word "Christian" and the apparent reluctance of those who first believed to accept it as a word to describe themselves. He also considers

- the use of the word "saints" to describe believers,
- the message they preached and believed,
- and their consequent witness in word and life.

Publications of The Open Bible Trust must be in accordance with its evangelical, fundamental and dispensational basis. However, beyond this minimum, writers are free to express whatever beliefs they may have as their own understanding, provided that the aim in so doing is to further the object of The Open Bible Trust. A copy of the doctrinal basis is available on **www.obt.org.uk** or from:

**THE OPEN BIBLE TRUST**
**Fordland Mount, Upper Basildon,**
**Reading, RG8 8LU, UK**